I0750268

FINISHING LINE PRESS
www.finishinglinepress.com

SORE POINTS

poems by

Kenneth Pobo

Finishing Line Press
Georgetown, Kentucky

SORE POINTS

ISBN 978-1-64662-759-2 First Edition

ACKNOWLEDGMENTS

Publisher: Leah Huete de Maines
Editor: Christen Kincaid
Author Photo: Stan Slater
Cover Design: Elizabeth Maines McCleavy

Order online: www.finishinglinepress.com
also available on amazon.com

Author inquiries and mail orders:
Finishing Line Press
P. O. Box 1626
Georgetown, Kentucky 40324
U. S. A.

Table of Contents

1. Aunt Gwen

Aunt Gwen And Her Name 1
Aunt Gwen Hiding 2
Aunt Gwen With The Thermometer 3
Aunt Gwen Sneaking 4
Aunt Gwen As Kite 5
Kites Over Branches 6
Red Ducks And A Bike 7
Aunt Gwen Learns To Drive 8
Aunt Gwen At Filene's The Running Of The Brides 9
Aunt Gwen Bastes The Turkey 10
Delia Anne At The Window 11
Aunt Gwen Caving 12
Aunt Gwen's Bubbles 13
Floribunda Gwen 14
About Her Marriage 15
Andy Williams 16
Aunt Gwen Forgives Little 17
About To Burst 18
Aunt Gwen's Evolution 19
Aunt Gwen Sneaks 20
Angelic Grapefruit 21
Aunt Gwen Tellin' It 22
Aunt Gwen Told Me, In Confidence 23
Aunt Gwen Lost 24
Aunt Gwen's Art History Lesson 25
Aunt Gwen's Ash Decade 26
Aunt Gwen's Close-Up 27
We Can't Convince Aunt Gwen 28
Aunt Gwen's Lopsidedness 29
Aunt Gwen's Weathervane 30
Aunt Gwen's Secretions 31
Caterpillar 32
Aunt Gwen In Winter 33
Aunt Gwen And The Juke Box 34
Aunt Gwen Without Fences 35
Seed Packets 36

II. Spacker

Spacker on Good ... 41
Spacker's Crayons ... 42
Spacker's Needle ... 43
Spacker's Match ... 44
On My List ... 45
Spacker Railway ... 46
Spacker Losing ... 47
Spacker Over Beers ... 48
Spacker's Bad Luck ... 49
Spacker's Car Concert ... 50
Spacker Is ... 51
Spacker Is So Tough ... 52
Spacker Used To ... 53
Spacker's Geology ... 54
Spacker Buries A Ring ... 55
Spacker Considers Moving To The City ... 56
Mix Master ... 57
On Cinder Blocks ... 58
Spacker Imagines Himself In *Whatever Happened To Baby Jane?* ... 59
Spacker Watches The Late Show ... 60
Spacker's Own ... 61
Spacker And Tomato Soup ... 62
Spacker Believes In God, But ... 63
Spacker Drinking ... 64
Spacker Looks Under ... 65
Spacker Begins ... 66
Blowing Stuff Up ... 67
Cosmology ... 68
Indolent Spacker ... 69
The Kid Spacker Hated ... 70
Pool Spacker ... 71
King Spacker ... 72
Sons ... 73
Someday Hair ... 74
What Must Come ... 75
November Spacker ... 76
Spacker Packing ... 77
Spacker Revisits Micah ... 78

For Stan

1. Aunt Gwen

AUNT GWEN AND HER NAME

1. Gwendolyn

Mom named me and ever since I was five or so I wanted to change it. Think of everything I'd have to update: licenses, cards, legal documents. It's better to be Gwendolyn but never call myself that.

I wasn't named after anybody, no bizarre but charming grandma getting pulled out of the grave and onto my name. Mom just thought it sounded elegant. She pictured me getting into movies. Grace Kelly. June Allyson. Gwendolyn Kleege. In our family acting was common. Every holiday everyone acted. Kiss, kiss. Bye.

Gwendolyn doesn't much like Gwen. She'd like Gwen to hold her head a bit higher, to get a divorce, and to take longer naps. Gwen tries to please too much.

2. Gwen

Sometimes my pals call me Gwenny, which I loathe, so they do it more. Usually I'm just Gwen. I don't know any famous Gwen's. I've read poems by Gwendolyn Brooks. One had "We die soon" or something in it. I may die soon. I'm 65 and still here.

I love a good time but keep a clean house. Try that when you live with Tree, a man who leaves dirty glasses in every room, drops his underwear anywhere he pleases, and do you think he lifts a finger to help? I could leave him, should leave him, I don't think I love him, but he's reliable, like an old credenza.

Gwen doesn't much like Gwendolyn. She'd like Gwendolyn to muss up her hair, tone down the make-up, and nap. Gwendolyn tries to please too much—herself.

AUNT GWEN HIDING

On the family farm, Gwen
would hide in the barn
or apple orchard. "Daddy
was mean," she says.
"He used a belt." She avoided

his funeral, angering her mother
who died skittery and bitter. Gwen
had learned how to escape
their grimaces—to locate
a perfect hiding place,
sometimes

on a busy street or in a bar
where pitchfork voices
can't prod her.

AUNT GWEN WITH THERMOMETER

I only played nurse and doctor
with one boy, Eric Clamp. I wanted

to be the doctor but he refused.
We showed what we didn't have.

I didn't want to play again.
Eric did. I heard he got divorced

twice. Did his wives want to be
the doctor and stubborn Eric insisted

that they play the game his way? Tree
tried that, ended up sleeping

on a basement sofa. These childhood sex
games are more like Biology class,

just you and another student,
no teacher. I blurted a question to

my folks about the penis. Mom
called it a "thing." Dad sank deeper

into the Lazy Boy. Eric and I got
placed in different 5th grade classes.

In junior high his family moved
to Santa Claus, Indiana. I got

interested in boys and girl groups—
did the Shangrilahs know everything?

Dating. The doctor is in.
The nurse stepped out for a bite.

AUNT GWEN SNEAKING

Her mother told her: *You're sixteen—*
get rid of it.
The neighbors are already
talking. Think of it
as a cigarette
you smash out.

Aunt Gwen didn't smoke.
Then.

Her folks hid her
in some Tennessee
unwed joint. She never saw

her child after she returned
to Antigo—her father
called her a whore

and her mother built
a fence made of guilt

which Gwen kept
sneaking through.

AUNT GWEN AS KITE

In my fifties, my friends try
to guess where our lives went

wrong, or if not wrong,
the many sidetracks that left us
tearing up old maps. Maybe
I should have left Illinois,
gone west, but I had parents

to take care of, a teetering job,
a daughter who often ran away—
I look for a magic kite,
charge after it despite bad knees,
a chronic wheeze,

and a windless summer
having no heft.

KITES OVER BRANCHES

In second grade Miss Rogers put Gwen in the yellow reading group. Learning to read came slowly, words rolling on her tongue like gumballs. How could she tell Miss Rogers that the books she was given bored her silly? Sure, Spot runs. What else would he do?

Almost sixty years ago. Reading is now a snack eaten between customers or after the dishes are done or before bed. When her husband asks which book is her favorite she says "Something on Lincoln, I think." He can name, in order, his Top Ten. Every one is about World War II.

Aunt Gwen tells few people about the high-school afternoon when she burnt a copy of The Bible. It seemed fun at the time. She has no guilt. After all, it's not like there's not scads of them all over. She grinned as the white cover flamed yellow and red. At first the smell was like autumn leaves burning. It grew more sour.

She tells her daughter to read more.

"Trash those movie magazines and read something more fulfilling."

"Movies fulfill me," Delia Anne replies. "And music magazines."

Aunt Gwen thinks of herself as a book. The pages turn much too quickly now.

Soon they'll litter the lawn, amble down the street. Her sentences released, like kites breaking free of branches, flying over her sagging roof.

RED DUCKS AND A BIKE

The tap closes. The workday squeezes
her shoes, so much standing. Yet she likes

her customers, mostly. Barney was in tonight.
He's fun when he isn't slamming ex-wife Sue
or remembering the fifties, always better
than now. He tells a good joke and isn't
a bad drunk. Nancy stopped in too,
rasping out stories of old boyfriends,
maybe lies, maybe not, but told well.
Gwen brings them drinks.
Barney is Coors, Nancy an Old Fashioned.

After locking up, Gwen stands in
a harsh wind waiting for the bus,
one of four or five people riding.
When she gets off three blocks from home,
she knows that Tree will be asleep,
the TV on, pizza on the couch's arm. She
puts on wool pajamas with red ducks
on the top and bottom, can't drift off,
he's snoring again, but when she finally fades

she dreams of speeding on a bicycle,
no handlebars, no streets, just motion—
and no destination.

AUNT GWEN LEARNS TO DRIVE

If my teacher ordered me right,
I turned left. Had he said down,
I'd have gone up

which would have been fun.

Why hug a road when you could be
on a cloud? Roads make us believe
that life is stop start. Traffic lights
have only three colors. Why so stingy?

On a cloud, there's only drifting,
no cops to pull me over. I got my license
though the testing lady warned me
about my parallel parking skills. All that
geometry unnerved me. Would you

like to take a spin? We could ride all over
the county, stop at Dairy Queen,
each get a dipped cone, I'll pay, and drive
to New Colony Park. Everything,

everything blooming. The car,
smelling of gas and lilacs,
will rise to clouds. Jack Benny performing
on a cumulus stage, Joan of Ark
kansas burning up a raindrop.

AUNT GWEN AT FILENE'S THE RUNNING OF THE BRIDES

When her Aunt Dora died, unexpectedly, Gwen, engaged, happy and worried, flew out to Brooklyn for the funeral. She wanted the perfect wedding dress, pictured Dora in Heaven, fanning herself because even in glory she would never feel cool enough. To please her guests, Gwen wanted to outdo splendid.

Even still, she thought to herself, "Weddings are mirages. We walk in the desert and think we find water, or a perfect dress, but it all goes poof."

She took the subway to Manhattan, camped out over night, knew the women who showed up may be sugar water at home become mambas when the doors open.

Gwen ran with the best of them, stripped in packed aisles, tried on what she could grab. It sounded like 3000 people in a box of Crackerjack a child shook.

The trouble with perfection is that excellence stinks. It just isn't good enough. While the brides lined up to pay, dejected Gwen left empty handed.

Shoulders slumped, she walked back to the subway, pictured Dora, dead but disappointed, and pews stuffed with relatives and friends looking at her like she just landed on Boardwalk, a hotel on it, no money in her account.

AUNT GWEN BASTES THE TURKEY

and thinks about how Delia Anne
stood apart from the other playgrounders:
Mommy, can we go home now?
The sun, a gold stick. Delia Anne's winter coat
hung like fog on her shoulders. Gwen told her,
Go and play. Look at the other children.
The child looked and ran to the fence.

Thirty years later, it's Thanksgiving
and her daughter has returned
from oily Mayflower, Arkansas,
her husband Ash having left her
for a Pascagoula woman who found
The Lord, dumped Ash who came
crawling back but she too had found
the Lord and got a job
in a Christian book store, dousing Ash
in prayers and guilt. Gwen liked him
until Pascagoula. Grief and fear

set the table. The future usually takes
the end seat, the place of honor.
This year there's an empty chair there,
no need to save the dark meat. Gray sky

knocks at the porch door. Loudly.
No one answers.

DELIA ANNE AT THE WINDOW

Mother is like a window
that I have to break. I stand
outside and shout. She won't hear
behind thick rain-stained panes.
She nags that I should be more grateful.
After all, they worked hard to give me
a place to live for a quarter of a century.

I am grateful.

I am also a stone hurtling
toward the window.
When it breaks,
who will clean up the shards?
Who will get new glass?

AUNT GWEN CAVING

Gwen had a fight on the phone
with her daughter, who just got canned.
She'll come home to live,
the fourth time. Gwen

mulls this over in Luray Caverns,
her friends Carla and Mandy walking
behind her, scared of falling
stalactites. Delia Anne,

made of mercury, appears,
disappears, often at the same time.
Cave-deep, the guide cuts the lights,
invites a beautiful and terrifying

darkness. All she sees
is Delia Anne's face in seventh grade,
her half-smile and nervous eyes.
The light returns. A collective

release of breath. Squinting,
they enter sunlight, buy cones,
talk about being young mothers
in babushkas and open-toe flats.

FLORIBUNDA GWEN

Tree says I do everything wrong.
I make fried chicken better
than anyone in the family,
which he won't admit. He calls me

a lousy driver, "like all women,"
has five tickets, points up the wazoo.
I can parallel park on a dime.
He can't even make the driveway

without wounding our forsythia.
Often I'd like to run him over,
nail his carcass to an exit ramp.
I won't. I'm like an ant

in an ice cube. I can't move.
Besides, sometimes he gives me
eleven roses, says I'm the twelfth—
he stole that

from a Hank Williams Jr. record,
but still.... Maybe
he'll get plunked in jail
for bad driving, call me to get him out—

I'll be too busy, a floribunda
scent wafting from the kitchen
window, roses fully open
in my grandmother's vase.

AUNT GWEN'S BUBBLES

At 11:55 Gwen hands Tree
the champagne—

when he pulls the cork,
the drink barely fizzes
over the bottle's lip. A few
bubbles break on her tongue.
Tree downs it in a swallow.

A glittery ball falls in
New York. Here,
two rings stain the coffee table.

A head with no face, the cork
rolls onto the floor, disappears
under a tippy couch.

ABOUT HER MARRIAGE

Thanksgiving. She wants the wings. I could fight her for them, but it's fun watching the pleasure she gets from tearing into them. A woman with royal molars. Tree can't join us this year. He's got the mumps—at 62.

Mom pours her usual bitter coffee and brings out a cake that looks some somebody put icing on a Honda.

Aunt Gwen takes a sizeable hunk, says that her life with Tree has been taking the small pieces and oh, the fury when he leaves half of it on his plate.

ANDY WILLIAMS

Aunt Gwen plays his albums while
pushing a splintery mop
over crabby kitchen tiles. Andy
sings that he hears the music
from across the way. Gwen thinks
maybe she hears it too—only a cat
scratching in litter. She wishes

that just once Tree would have taken her
to see him at the Moon River Theater
in Branson. He promised,
but his job got busy and
Delia Anne came home broke.

As Gwen pours gray water down the sink,
Andy sings "Moon River"—
We're after the same rainbow's end,
the album turning in endless circles, Gwen

stopping suddenly when a tuxedo'd man
leaps out from worn grooves
to offer her one red rose.

AUNT GWEN FORGIVES LITTLE

On the spotty Sundays
when she goes to church, she dreads
hymns, thinks them tuneless

and childish. No clinging to
an old rugged cross for her—
she never clings, says prayers

if they're short and not booby-trapped
with supplications. She likes
that Jesus can forgive. At least

somebody can! Sometimes
she wishes that he'd return
right this minute and smite a lot

of nasty people. Usually
she's glad that he's in heaven
so she's still got time to wash

the basement windows and
put three old blouses in a bag
for the hospital resale shop.

ABOUT TO BURST

While enjoying the hell
out of Bette Davis in *Of Human Bondage,*
she wishes that she could wipe

Tree's kisses off her mouth
the way Davis does,
no she doesn't, she apologizes,
she loves her husband, really,
but will he ever pick up a glass
and put it in the sink? A riled
Davis would have kicked Tree.

Aunt Gwen crabs and cusses,
an M-80 about to burst
in a hand.

AUNT GWEN'S EVOLUTION

Pastor Blamp says we didn't
come from monkeys
while Deacon Trumblo scratches
his arm pit. What's so bad
about monkeys? Some women in

our sewing circle, Ruth's Gems,
say you can't believe in God
and evolution. Mary Pat
has a very unevolved husband
as do I, so she may be right.

I'm not all that evolved. I'm 60
going on 14. I hoped to be

a sudoku, all figured out by now.

AUNT GWEN SNEAKS

The service begins promptly at 11:00,
the hour of the week that Gwen most hates.
She thinks that she's hard ground,
the church members a trowel, scratching
to open her up. She has spent half a century
trying to please. Her Uncle Jim is tough to please
though many call him a "loving spirit."

Hymns done, the morning prayer said,
Jim grabs the pulpit as if it's a football
he's going to toss into the end zone.

Gwen pulls a screen over herself
in the front pew, changes clothes.
Jim leads twenty-four souls in a prayer
that can also be used for tanning lotion.
In a bikini, Gwen stretches out. The sun breaks
through stained glass and kisses her.
Pelicans and cockatoos roost
on the organ bench.

A minute
before he is ready to invite people up to accept Christ,
Jim notices Gwen. Alarmed,
he keeps speaking. It's important not to make a scene,
to do things in the promised order. He can't resist—

blocked by the pulpit, Jim calls to her,
calls to her, calls to her.

ANGELIC GRAPEFRUIT

While she carves a grapefruit,
juice squirts in her eye.

The Angel Marsha appears on rinds,
licks honey off the plastic bear.

Tony, her favorite angel, rides a bike
and, like a baseball card in spokes,
his cht-cht comforts Gwen
when bills come and come

or when a phone call scuttles in
while Ellen's show celebrates
TV moms. Alert, her angels rise
when they hear a rumble,

her furnace dying again.
On a Sunday.

AUNT GWEN TELLIN' IT

My dreams are like Japanese
beetles eating holes into a just
bloomed white hibiscus. You think
that if my dreams come "true"
then I'll be pulled up from a river
that I never jumped into. Dreams
beget dreams. And nightmares.

I thought I wanted to marry,
to have kids. That one came "true"—
it's like a nighttime dream I have
where all my teeth fall out.
 I wake up
 sweaty.

AUNT GWEN TOLD ME, IN CONFIDENCE,

that in a previous life she
was Joan Crawford, a shop girl,
a no one can stop girl
who became a star. She glided
down an elegant staircase
in a black gown,
a pearl necklace,
heard L.B. Mayer say,
"Joan, don't you look lovely!"

Aunt Gwen bartended
at Cal's Tap, died a pauper.
L. B. Mayer was really
a customer banging his tumbler
on the bar. She never
visited Hollywood

but kept an autographed picture
of Crawford in in her desk—
on top of the one
of her daughter's prom.

AUNT GWEN LOST

A forest deepens, the path unclear.
Night darkens the green

question marks of ferns. Out of
a declining blue, the road reappears.

I'm not found, but I know, somewhat,
where to walk—

hope curves in a headlight, slides
up from a worm's hungry mouth.

AUNT GWEN'S ART HISTORY LESSON

She says that when Rembrandt painted
the *Mona Lisa*
he had an out-of-body experience

and actually became Mona.
Maybe so. Sometimes while singing
in the shower, my body disappears.

Notes pull me up through the showerhead
and out to the town square of my childhood,
now a Wal-Mart. I break the news to my sister

that da Vinci painted it. She says
she was just testing me: was I listening?
I passed. This time.

She tests us often. Usually we flunk.
She wishes that we would improve,
smiles like Mona when we scram.

AUNT GWEN'S ASH DECADE

My sister Gert warned me: *Some day*
the rug will be pulled right out
from under you. She'd have done it

herself had she lived nearer. Turns out
I didn't need Gert. I opened the door,
and a decade died in my arms.

My husband had an affair.
Several affairs. Our daughter
stole from her employer, ended up
in jail. I got fired from Cal's Tap.
A customer said I was Job waiting
for boils. Job got a new family,
prestige. I stayed with Tree
who promised no more women.
I knew he was lying. Delia Anne moved

back in, might go to Bible college.
I became a Red Lobster server. Don't
believe those who say, "It all worked out.
You survived." Look at my face.
My eyes are burnt cellophane. My lips,
severe gashes. My soul you can't see—

I learned how to hide that so well
that even I can't find it anymore.

AUNT GWEN'S CLOSE-UP

In the picture that I insisted
you take, I'm squinting.
It's like I'm trying to make out

who you are or could be.
Not angry or happy, I look
like a secret got caught

in my throat that I can't
cough out. Maybe next time
you'll pose me in the shade—

I'll have a smile deep
as Lake Superior. You'll snap
just at the moment when

my secret gets free, leaves me
grinning like a woman who
got locked in her own garage

but now walks away or
like a woman who just realizes
she's lost everything.

WE CAN'T CONVINCE AUNT GWEN

to get a computer. She says modern things
break her heart. When we bought her
a washing machine, she feigned interest,
then treated it as a table and kept using
her roller washer, which, she insists,
cleans clothes better. And a dishwasher?
Forget it. Her hands know her plates
and glasses better. Why take a chance?

A concession: she has a color TV, mostly
because she can't find a decent black and white
anymore, to her unyielding anger. Color
makes the people look like refugees
from a bad trip, she pouts. She'd go
to movies if they were silent except for

the piano. She's only in her mid-60s,
not that conservative. She usually
votes Democrat. But she mistrusts most
of what's gone down in the past
hundred years, bemoans what she calls
the ever-sharpened pencils of darkness.

Sometimes I think she's right. I've seen
what those pencils write—it isn't pretty.

AUNT GWEN'S LOPSIDEDNESS

You can say what you want about her—and people say plenty. Several planets took root in her spine. This makes her wobble, but not terribly. Gwen's laugh causes sunspots. Satellites quiver when she hears a joke she likes, usually one about the rich. Not rich herself, except in planets, she can never unload a single one at Baby Jane's Pawn Shop.

AUNT GWEN'S WEATHERVANE

"Make something beautiful,"
my grandmother said,
in a colorless-sky apron.

Beauty? To her, a homemade cake,
one too good to sell at the church auction.
To me, Colorado's autumn aspens
we saw on our honeymoon.
I barely remember the honeymoon.
I can't make an aspen's yellow fire
burning up a mountainside. I can make
a joyful noise when I sing along
with Michael Buble in the shower.
Making something beautiful
may take a lifetime, several—

or, does it come in a second, urgent,
a meteor striking a weathervane,
everything changed, even me.

AUNT GWEN'S SECRETIONS

We invite her over once a year, a day we dread. On the glider she talks about my other aunts, all three of them failures, even Aunt Wag who invented silent flush birthday candles. She doesn't say what she thinks of us, but she sighs, shakes her head, and looks away.

A bizarre goo that smells like iodine floats out of her pores. I say nothing, just get her summer sausage on a Ritz cracker that she eats in one bite, the floor getting sticky.

CATERPILLAR

While Aunt Gwen sits on
the stiff-backed gold chair,
which she calls "ostentatious,"
a caterpillar crawls up
from her neck and into
her stiff-backed gold hair.

She doesn't brush it away.

When I ask why, she tells me
that all her life she has been waiting
for a butterfly to spring
out from her.
And flex,

orange and black wings
making gray roofs disappear.

AUNT GWEN IN WINTER

Snow, a tightrope walker,
tiptoes from the chimney
to the top of our elm. I keep
waiting for him to fall

and die. My husband wouldn't notice,
sighs in his boxers. I don't sigh much.
I scream at the window,
tell a hostile wind to stop blowing
at once. It never listens.

Margie at the bar listens,
says I'm wasting my life.
I should be wearing mauve mumus
where strangers drink margaritas
on glass-bottomed boats.

The faucet needs a washer.
I'll leave the water dripping
tonight. The pipes might freeze.
Something terrible hides
in my sweater.

AUNT GWEN AND THE JUKE BOX

She never gets the song she's looking for,
goes from title to title—
the rhythm's off, the beat
loses punch. She's beginning
to lose interest in music.

It's dawning on her that
she can dance without it.

AUNT GWEN WITHOUT FENCES

At the end of her life, she sees
warm light that smells
like Jesus and datura. Gwen

feels like her personal history
is being replayed across
the universe. Decisions
she made have different outcomes.
She walks in a garden
of protons. All fences,

everywhere,
have vanished.

SEED PACKETS

For my birthday, Spacker
bought me 20 seed packets
at the dime store. "I know you

like flowers, Aunt Gwen" he said,
before kicking the back door open
and getting into that Oldsmobile

Cutlass he restored, well,
he says he restored it,
I've made cakes that fell

and claimed that I was trying
to bake flatter cakes. Icing
hides everything. Spacker's

a failure, I don't mean this
unkindly, he'd agree, failure
works well as long as Dora

brings him a beer and the Cutlass
chugs him back home where
Gert makes him a 7-Up

float before he goes to bed,
even though he's 28, but he's right,
I do like flowers. I'll tear off

the packet tops, drop the seeds
in my mixing bowl, and plant them
on sunny dirt beside the trash cans—

something might come up,
stem surprises,
a small way to restore summer.

II. Spacker

SPACKER ON GOOD

Uncle Tree doesn't hand out compliments—everything is done wrong, a mess-up. Don't get him started on the government: Republican or Democrat, they're all kooks out to get him. The whole family's out to get him. He told Aunt Gwen that if he could get away with it, he'd poison us all at Thanksgiving and wouldn't even clean up afterwards. He was joking, maybe. Aunt Gwen's used to it, but mom says she sleeps with a carving knife in the top drawer of her side of the bed. I doubt that. Tree and Gwen haven't shared a bed since Nero. I may be Uncle Tree's secret bastard. Not that mom would ever do something like that (Tree's her bro-in-law for Pete's sake) but I could easily set the house on fire when everyone's chattering away, arguing over the virtues of vanilla or chocolate cake, shouting curses at a TV screen when some "crucial" game demands a loser. I'm a loser, yeah, sure am. Frank Sinatra and Ava Gardner got divorced. You can have stacks of money and still the good slips away. Which it will do. Because it is good. And it runs off.

SPACKER'S CRAYONS

I lug a boulder,
drop it on a still pond,
bored when ripples fade.
This craving to bust
things up, I know
it's trouble—most
people here live
like boxed crayons.
I melt crayons.
Colors blend
and reharden into
something no one has
ever seen before.

SPACKER'S NEEDLE

Sneakers muddy from rainy grass,
Spacker grinds in footprints
on his mother's washed floor,

giggles. She yells so Spacker
does it again. She asks Father Wink
to come over—he calls him "My son,"
so Spacker pulls out his BB gun.
Father escapes through a side door.

Crick applauds, preferring bike tires
to church. Spacker farts
right in his face.

It's like he was born
holding a needle, ready
to stitch up a world he already knew
was fatally torn—he dropped

the needle and tore it
as hard as he could.

SPACKER'S MATCH

What kind of match would set
the world on fire? Can one guy

be strong enough to blaze
the whole stupid thing? Millions
transform themselves into
a human firetruck—
only it arrives too late. The planet,
a big smoke pit.

The fire—how grand, lapping up clouds,
burning a marshmallow moon.

He goes to work at Swanee's Pizza Pad.
Oven fires melt the cheese,
make tomato sauce sizzle. He sweats ferociously,
a hell, a kind of happy hell.

ON MY LIST

Whenever Spacker gets angry,
and that's almost all the time,
he finds a culprit, says,

"You're on my list!"
This long list includes
the dead. He thinks of his

list as a broken-down bus
rusting five miles out of town
in Kregar's field. Someday

everyone on it will end up
in that bus. The people,
even God, will spend the rest

of their lives looking
out of broken windows,
eating smelly bag lunches,

Spacker sitting in
the driver's seat trying
to start the engine again

and again, but it's too
far gone. The traveling
salesman sky has no clients.

SPACKER RAILWAY

Spacker thinks of people in Micah as train track ties. How fun when the train chugs by and kills them. He wishes he were the engineer. Here, people pass time—in beauty parlors, ammo shops, malls and bars. Until the grave robs them. Spacker doesn't pass time—he licks it like a Reese's peanutbutter cup, though the sweet taste always goes away. That's when he heads for the depot to wait for the train he never boards. He cusses if it's late. When it comes, having killed everyone but him, he waves at the engineer who waves back.

SPACKER LOSING

Sometimes I think I should quit cards,
try something sensible like roulette,

the ball dizzying around in a circle,
a safer bet. Dad says the house

always wins. Funny,
our house never wins, can barely

stand up. No one has the gumption
to paint it. All that tax money

piling up in Jeff City, no wonder
Missouri can bend luck

to its whims. Nothing bends
for me except the highway's

shoulder which my truck sits on
while I read a map I got

at a Welcome Center that shows me
the many ways I can go to leave

this state, the many ways
that return me to it.

SPACKER OVER BEERS

He often imagines curves
of women, the smell

of their hair, the usual places
that excite him. But he spits

out jokes about their brains,
their driving. In Kelly's Bar,

he tries to pick up
a woman, any woman,

calls her a *bitch*
when she leaves.

SPACKER'S BAD LUCK

Spacker and his Aunt Gwen walk out of the Micah Walmart. He almost bought another gun, his family has 80 already, but Aunt Gwen says she won't loan him the money.

"You're a stupid old bitch," he says.
"And you aren't worthy to tie my shoes."

To Spacker, Missouri is like a fished-out lake. Prairies and farms make him feel as if he's a carcass, ants crawling all over it.

"Have a great day, folks," the Walmart greeter, Ted Kompleman, says as they leave. He's 83, has a smile like a half-filled bike tire.

A bee flies into Spacker's mouth. He swallows it.

"There ain't any good days here," Spacker grumbles as he and his aunt head for the truck.

SPACKER'S CAR CONCERT

Driving, windows open, he doesn't
care who hears him,
not that anyone would on Highway 19.
He starts with "Big Yellow Taxi,"
which he calls "a tree-hugging song"
but it nests under his scalp. He

veers into "All Falls Down," pretends
he's Kanye, though he hates hiphop
even when it kisses his tongue.
Finally it's "Lullabye of Broadway"—
he sees himself on stage looking very
1935 surrounded by babes who'd
never glance twice at him in Micah

where kids spit watermelon seeds
at the water tower, where
old farmers sit on town square
benches and talk about why
schools shouldn't teach evolution.

Spacker arrives in Eminence,
hometown of astronaut Tom Akers,
a guy who knew that getting
away from Earth is a great way
to learn how to sing.

SPACKER IS

a disgusting pig
says Marianne Salodner to Dorian Lord—

Spacker had promised to marry her,
shot a twelve-point buck instead.
Dorian wants Spacker too—
Micah's men aren't much,
and Spacker at least isn't drunk

half the time, maybe. He likes
disgusting pigs, wrestled one to a draw
at the county fair. How could

marriage be better than wrestling
a pig? Why not stay single—
if the bed is cold,
it's no colder than getting up
at 4:30 to hunt in an orange jacket.

Life is pretty cold anyway. You see
your breath. Briefly.

SPACKER IS SO TOUGH

that when Doug The Slug attacks
his patriotism, he swallows three
large nails right at the bar. Doug's
unimpressed, but only men who keep
many women on a string impress him.
Doug hasn't had a girlfriend in almost
a decade, says that *I'm too tough*
for women to handle. Spacker

devours women like Butterfingers
candy bars. They're tasty and fun—
then he goes back to the shooting range

or tap. At the hospital, Dr. Barnick
removes the nails. Spacker gives him
a wet willy and leaves. Doug The Slug

stops insulting Spacker, won't even
talk to him—and drinks his St. Pauli Girl
at a table behind the juke box,
the wobbly one that the waitress
Dorene often forgets.

SPACKER USED TO

pretend puffy dandelions
were old men in a hospital,
he, the doctor who scissors
their heads off. Grown up,

when he sees a dandelion,
the yellow face a huge grin,
he grinds it deep into dirt,
drives to Sonic for a burger,
flirts with Dina, the carhop,

with her dangerous
yellow beehive.

SPACKER'S GEOLOGY

Spacker doesn't want to leave Missouri—except for one place: The Big Island of Hawaii where lava oozes redly to the sea, drops in, makes steam. He'd like to be lava, ocean, and steam. At the same time. At home he's a fork, a knife, and a spoon on a table where he is no longer welcome to eat.

SPACKER BURIES A RING

When I gave Joy a ring
in 8th grade, she rolled it
like a small bowling ball
down the hall. I thought
she liked me. We talked
in Language Arts. Later

I learned that she thought
I was nice—
but a loser
from a bad family. I rescued
the ring from the janitor's pail,
stored it in the attic. Packing

to move out, there it was,
yellow tin, alone, needing
a finger that would never come.

I buried it
in the back yard,
pretended to be a priest,
sprinkled oak leaves over it,
cursed Joy who, I've heard,

has a ring
that she removes
when her trucker husband
goes out of town.

SPACKER CONSIDERS MOVING TO THE CITY

He dreams that he's Samson
pulling the town pillars down,
no Delilah, few friends
unless a rifle is a friend. His brother
Crick grunts that pigs have it good—

they don't have to work,
get fattened up, and no one rags
on a pig for being sloppy. Spacker's
vaguely sloppy in worn jeans
and garage-sale shirts that make him

look like an old man. In Joplin
maybe he could find a girl
who knows taxidermy, who wouldn't
talk back, just get his dinner,
be warm in bed, and look pretty

on his arm. His mother says
good luck with that. Spacker says
his mother will miss him when he moves.
He'll never invite her to visit,
his wife might, though the way

things go, he thinks it'll end in
a divorce, and maybe, if his luck turns,
a cheap used truck to buy
and pancakes that get a fine thin crust
and don't burn.

MIX MASTER

“For your tenth birthday, “I’m gonna microwave you and twirl your soggy brains in the mix master,” Spacker told his brother.

Laughing, Crick thought his older brother was a scream.

“You won’t neither. You need me to play P-I-G with.”

“Wait and see.”

When Spacker killed Crick, he found killing to be a kick. Causing “accidents” was fun. He sought out Dora who said Crick was better in the sack. He figured he could make her eat something poisonous, a sugary death treat.

An ambulance hauled her away like a bag of rotten turnips.

SPACKER IMAGINES HIMSELF STARRING IN *WHATEVER HAPPENED TO BABY JANE?*

He's seen the film 30 times at least, knows his favorite bits of dialogue the way his mother knows verses in *Galatians.* Ask him why he likes the film so much and he shrugs. Peek at him when he's watching it and see how he smiles when Bette Davis kicks Joan Crawford at the bottom of the stairs or when Jane serves Blanche a rat.

His brother Crick thinks most movies are dumb, prefers NASCAR, beer, and Hooters. The other guys want action films and sports vids. Spacker likes those too,

but at night before he falls asleep he thinks his brother is Blanche. He makes plans: tape over the lips, rope around the wrists. His brother looking almost angelic in his sleep.

ON CINDER BLOCKS

Spacker never admits to anyone that he killed Crick who sprawled under the '77 Buick when the car "accidentally" fell off the cinder blocks. Spacker got loads of sympathy.

"He was my only bro," he said, "almost a god to me."

Crick bedded any girl who would have him—including two of Spacker's girlfriends—his high school sweetheart Dina Rose and a girl named Dora who he met at a 7-11 and dated for six months.

Spacker grinned at the crack of his brother's rib cage as the car fell, the sound of death swimming up Crick's breath.

Even though all of Micah Township thought the brothers were close, he never liked Crick. Even at age five, Spacker took a fork and stabbed him in the belly. Crick shrieked. Terrific fun!

The Buick ended up crumpled in a ditch. The Bailey Boys had stolen it and pushed it off the cliff. That's when Spacker cried. He carried the steering wheel home, the closest thing to a baby he thought he'd ever have.

SPACKER WATCHES THE LATE SHOW

Midnight and a movie alone.
Bette Davis tells Paul Henreid
that they shouldn't ask for the moon
when they have the stars. Spacker

wants the moon too, would stuff
the solar system in his backpack
and traipse from one diner
to another. Sometimes he wishes
that he were a star, name in lights,
giving interviews. In Micah,

few even wave to him. He knows
they think he's funny, I mean,
was it an accident that he killed
his brother? Was it an accident
when he set Sophie's hair on fire
before the prom? The Late Show

tucks him into bed, spilled Fritos
on unfluffed pillows, a coughing
pick-up truck lullabye
with nervous verses.

SPACKER'S OWN

Mom, a cooking robot, easily programmed,
says now I'm "on my own."
My own what? I rent my furniture.
The lease goes month to month.

Before I moved out, she gave me
two pans and some weird thing
to stir junk inside an egg.
I burn hot dogs, not sure how,
watch the Cards instead. My girlfriend

Ashley hands me a recipe she got
off Wikipedia for steak au poivre,
expects a Saturday dinner for two—
I don't eat what I can't pronounce.
Marriage? I'd rather be a hydrant,
a spaniel coming toward me.

SPACKER AND TOMATO SOUP

As his lips redden
he remembers his dad planting
tomato seedlings in warm dirt—
everything had to be just right
or there'd be nothing to slop up
your July face. Spacker

rarely misses his parents,
didn't attend either funeral,
but when he thinks of rich
tomato soup, he stops turning
Time's pages, pictures red waves,

his mom's finger in *Second Kings*,
his dad screaming at the sports section.

SPACKER BELIEVES IN GOD, BUT

His God shows himself to be real
when a gun fires.
In the richochet Spacker finds God.

His mother thinks Spacker's
an atheist. She frets that his soul
will be a leaf burning
forever. Ask him and he'll tell you

he hates atheists, thinks
they should be shot.
By his God.

Then they would know the truth.

SPACKER DRINKING

at the springs of living water,
the last hymn he remembers
mumbling in church. The next week
he quit going.

Bills, failing farms, drought
followed by floods—Heaven
got pneumonia. Worshippers expect
a do-over in the next life. Spacker
thinks that no one makes
everything alright. At thirty,

he killed two deer, the buck's head
on his bedroom wall. Dead eyes
watch him sleep. What forests
would they roam in Glory?

In leather boots that he garbage picked,
he walks to the Warrenton Waffle House,
eats syrup-embalmed sausages,
tears open soggy sugar packets.

A table away, his former Pastor's family
stabs golden waffles.

SPACKER LOOKS UNDER

rocks, thinks he'll find something
splendid. Most of his life has come up
snake eyes. The more he tried to win

playing it fair and square, the more teeth
cracked in fights. His friend Danny the Raunch
found a wedding ring under a boulder

by Syssygy Creek. He gave it to his girlfriend
Wanda who was thrilled, who was pregnant,
who divorced him eight months later. Now

Danny sits on rocks,
doesn't look beneath them. Spacker will avoid
wedding rings. He might find

a small bank with a tiny teller offering him
millions of bucks. Or
a rattler, disturbed, aiming for his eyes.

SPACKER BEGINS

most mornings with Pop Tarts,
a strawberry blandness matched
by Orange Crush, better than

orange juice, better than sex. Well,
not better, but it requires less effort.
Spacker dislikes eating breakfast

with anyone. Alone is a smell
of butter seeping into an English muffin.
Dad calls him a grump. Mom looks

like the Virgin, heart pulled open.
His brother sees only guns and cars.
Ask him what day it is

and he'll say T-bucket. Spacker
gets ready for his latest job,
a landscape worker. He never

keeps them long. Arguments
are like bees. The boss swats him,
throws him away.

BLOWING STUFF UP

In the Micah library, Spacker looked at the Missouri map, two pages of despair, in an atlas. Mrs. Cripshaw watched patrons closely. A book thief could be in the three-room library. Or a teenager sneaking a smoke in the bathroom.

Spacker believed in hell, not heaven, and was sure that Mrs. Cripshaw would be damned to hell forever, mourning a world of card catalogues replaced by computers. She had assumed she was going to heaven, but here was Satan, checking out books that he had no intention of reading or returning. In fact, he was the best bookburner the world had ever known—impotent Mrs. Cripshaw could do nothing to stop him.

Micah was an hour south of Jeff City. He had a used truck, but rarely drove more than twenty miles from town, one that Satan never bothered to visit.

"When I blow this town, I'm leaving no survivors. They'll thank me," he said to no one, uneasy that he'd probably never leave. You don't leave hell.

Spacker would wave when he saw neighbors in the town square, but his ways and habits were pretty well known: He liked blowing stuff up. One time he gathered twenty-six buckets, turned them upside down, peed on each one, then took out his gun and shot them—all while laughing like a hyena. It didn't matter what it was, big or small, if Spacker could blow it up he would. For now, he left houses and stores alone, saving them for the Big Explosion on the day when he left town for good. In the mean time, he blew holes in electric fences, shot the heads off of daffodils, and everyone believed that Spacker was responsible for blowing up Mayor Adelle Turner's shed.

Risking Mrs. Cripshaw's nose and wrath, he lit a Marlboro in the back of the library and burned a hole in the atlas, burned Micah off the page, taking the county with it. Mrs. Cripshaw dashed over and tossed him out. He laughed, loudly, and she forbade him to ever return.

No problem. He didn't like reading anyway. Maybe it wouldn't be more than six months or so before he'd have enough explosives to ka-boom the library, Mrs. Cripshaw in it, red bricks tumbling from the sky like meteors falling all over town.

COSMOLOGY

Buds poured, Fritos half asleep,
Jack tells Spacker about anti-particles
as real to Jack as the wife who left him.

Jack worries about the universe—
what if it's open
and stars crap out, darken forever?

Cosmology bores Spacker
who prefers greasy guitars
and fishing lures. Knowing his temper,

few talk to Spacker. He might
explode, a star in a distant galaxy
frosting the bar with fire.

INDOLENT SPACKER

He's malevolent in any weather,
but when temperatures fire up,
he swings back and forth
for hours, lemonade sweating

in a glass, imagines a ruckus
he could create, the hell
he could raise
and lower. Upheaval

gives him a buzz
or something close to it.
Today he listens to birds
he barely watches

in the dogwood tree. When a spider
crawls on the porch wall,
he thinks he'd normally smash it,
but not now, not after

he swallows a yellow
sleeping pill sun
and drops against
a rickety door of dreams.

THE KID SPACKER HATED

In fifth grade, Spacker singled out
puny Carl Jopson who excelled
in American History, had red fright-wig hair
that Spacker would grab, pull and twist.

Mrs. Gent, his teacher, watched,
held her hat close to her head,
fearing gusts. Carl swore vengeance,
but during the summer his family moved
to Tennessee. Spacker found
new kids to slap or pin to a door.

To hurt was like breathing—
he just did it.

POOL SPACKER

swims for barely fifteen minutes,
drips to the changing room,
and steals flip-flops
or beach balls, knowing

some kid will be mightily upset—
he remembers when his mom
told him he couldn't ride his bike
for a week, he had sassed her,

and he got mightily upset too.
He tosses the flip-flops
in the back of his truck,
drives to Montrose Lake—

by the shore, old tires, condoms,
cigarette butts, and tracts
for Tryst Falls Baptist Church.
After he lights the flip-flops,

they smolder—he's got time,
what's there to do in Micah
but watch the night
cover cornfields in darkness

so it can pull the red
petals off of Mrs. Gutaway's
Mirandy rose, burning
rubber a comfort,

like a story he was told
when he was five
about a lightning bug
on a string that broke free.

KING SPACKER

Half drunk, he talks
to his friend DABO,
Dave August Braller,

that he'd like to be king.
Henry VIII could get rid of
wives when they outlived

their usefulness. As king
in Micah, he'd ban everyone,
walk into stores, no clerks—

take whatever he wants
for free. Soon he'd rule
the state, America,

the world until death performs
that single revolutionary act
and dethrones him.

SONS

For as long as he can remember, Spacker has hated his name. Bored one Saturday, he snuck over to Mr. Cawley's farm and painted it on his barn, each red letter like a bleeding lip. Nobody liked Mr. Cawley—he didn't go to church, rarely came to town, and when he did he looked straight ahead, never bothering to wave or say hi.

This made him A-OK in Spacker's book. He wished Mr. Cawley was his dad. Mr. Cawley would've made a rotten dad. He often threatened kids who got on his property and often said "Kids should be taken to the top of the water tower and pushed off. I'd gladly do it myself."

Kindly but blobbish, Spacker's own dad worked at Quick Stop, rubbed Spacker's head when he came home, said "Hiya kiddio," watched the sports channel and drank Pauli Girl beer until he fell asleep in the broken Lazy Boy. Spacker determined not to become him. Trouble was, he didn't know who to become and he was stuck with this stupid name.

When he shot each of the letters he had painted on Cawley's barn, Cawley charged out of his house, screaming, fist in the air. Like a kitten that suddenly loses its energy, he watched as Spacker reloaded, shooting now just for fun. As he looked at Spacker, he thought that his life would have been great if only he'd had a son.

SOMEDAY HAIR

Looking for pants, Spacker drifts
around the Men's Department,
finds any department irritating,
even the fire department, ends up

at Anna's Resale Shop.
Most pairs fit poorly, sag
like the front porch. He likes the older ladies
who take his 75 cents
and wish him a good day,

picks up Mary Ann from the Walmart
who thanks shoppers for stopping in,
her dress smelling like fried chicken
and Justin Bieber Someday Hair Mist.

WHAT MUST COME

Spacker won't walk under a ladder
or open an umbrella in his apartment.
His religion, luck.
You're born in Missouri or in Niger.
You make money or go broke.
Why risk?

Yet he gambles often,
never uses a condom,
eats bags of McDonald's fries,
smokes Kents,
swills Jim Beam. A black cat
crossing before him? He runs.

Staying on the alert,
he expects trouble,
7 years of it,

no way to stop what must come.

NOVEMBER SPACKER

My sixth-grade teacher, Mr. Drashal,
would write NOVEMBER on the board,

and read poems about death.

Our trees
finally drop parasite leaves, let them fall

and blow away. If only this town
would do that. Instead it burps

up a new Wal Mart. It's November
at last, dreary. Thanksgiving,

death on the table, everyone
ready to dig in.

SPACKER PACKING

I'm 33, not a happy ending
kind of guy. Neither are you.
Alive now, decay later.

Why turn to ash in a town
that should have burned
to the ground long ago?

I have no destination,
maybe Tennessee, it's got mountains
so good I could lick them

like gravy off a plate. If
moonlight shines at a good angle,
I'll stay there, for a while. I have

little to pack, hardly enough
to strain my back. My Aunt says
I'll regret leaving. I may.

I regret a lot. For now,
home will be acceleration,
the windshield leading me

straight ahead until curves dip.
I'll crumple the map,
toss it out of the window.

SPACKER REVISITS MICAH

A freshly painted sign
welcomes drivers into a town
of 1236 people and

12 churches. Micah's high school
hasn't quite collapsed yet. A town
square died into broken beer bottles

that pay homage to
the statue of W.D. Pengraft,
the founder.

I'm a washing machine
on a rickety porch used
only for holding an iced tea glass.

ACKNOWLEDGEMENTS

"Aunt Gwen And Her Name" 1-70 Review
"Aunt Gwen Hiding" Icon
"Aunt Gwen With The Thermometer" Eucalasia
"Aunt Gwen Sneaking" Broadkill Review
"Aunt Gwen As Kite" The Tau
"Kits Over Branches" Flash Frontier
"Red Ducks And A Bike" Agave
"Aunt Gwen Learns To Drive" Icon
"Aunt Gwen At Filene's" 1-70 Review
"Aunt Gwen Bastes The Turkey" Mojave River Review
"Delia Anne At The Window" Mojave River Review
"Aunt Gwen Caving" Blue Heron Review
"Aunt Gwen's Bubbles" Broadkill Review
"Floribunda Gwen" Transient Publishing
"About Her Marriage" Bat Terrier
"Andy Williams" Califragile
"Aunt Gwen Forgives Little" Rose & Thorn
"About To Burst" Broadkill Review
"Aunt Gwen's Evolution" Comstock Review
"Aunt Gwen Sneaks" Zodiac Review
"Angelic Grapefruit" Broadkill Review
"Aunt Gwen Tellin' It" Eclectica
"Aunt Gwen Told Me, In Confidence" This Zine Will Change Your Life
"Aunt Gwen Lost" Hollow
"Aunt Gwen's Art History Lesson" Houston Nomadic Voices
"Aunt Gwen's Ash Decade" ABZ
"Aunt Gwen's Close-Up" Rabbit
"We Can't Convince Aunt Gwen" The First Cut
"Aunt Gwen's Lopsidedness" Six Sentences
"Aunt Gwen's Weathervane" Broadkill Review
"Aunt Gwen's Secretions" Sand
"Caterpillar" Barefoot Review
"Aunt Gwen And The Juke Box" Lost Coast Review
"Aunt Gwen Without Fences" Montucky Review
"Seed Packets" Broadkill Review
"Spacker On Good" Broadkill Review
"Spacker's Crayons" Lost Coast Review

"Spacker's Needle" Pure Francis
"Spacker's Match" Up The River
"On My List" Zombie Logic
"Spacker Railway" Marco Polo
"Spacker Over Beers" Subterranean Quarterly
"Spacker's Bad Luck" Piedmont Journal
"Spacker's Car Concert" Broadkill Review
"Spacker Is" Rufous City Review
"Spacker Is So Tough" Kenning Journal
"Spacker Used To" Ishaan Literary Review
"Spacker Buries A Ring" Pittsburgh Poetry Journal
"Spacker Considers Moving To The City" Broadkill Review
"Mix Master" Flashshot
"On Cinder Blocks" Apocrypha & Abstractions
"Spacker Imagines Himself" Icon
"Spacker Watches The Late Show" Piedmont Journal
"Spacker's Own" Broadkill Review
"Spacker And Tomato Soup" Up The River
"Spacker Believes In God, But" Zombie Logic
"Spacker Drinking" Broadkill Review
"Spacker Looks Under" Cordite Poetry Review
"Spacker Begins" Canyon Voices
"Blowing Stuff Up" Apocrypha & Abstractions
"Cosmology" Katerskill Basin
"Indolent Spacker" Ray's Road Review
"The Kid Spacker Hated" Up The River
"Pool Spacker" Ray's Road Review
"King Spacker" Califragile
"Sons" Echolocation
"Someday Hair" Broadkill Review
"What Must Come" Broadkill Review
"November Spacker" Cordite Poetry Review
"Spacker Packing" Potluck Magazine
"Spacker Revisits Micah" Zombie Logic

Kenneth Pobo is the author of twenty-one chapbooks and nine full-length collections. In addition to *Sore Points* (FLP), recent books include *Bend of Quiet* (Blue Light Press), *Loplop in a Red City* (Circling Rivers), and *Uneven Steven* (Assure Press). His work has appeared in *North Dakota Quarterly, Nimrod, Mudfish, Hawaii Review,* and elsewhere.

www.ingramcontent.com/pod-product-compliance
Lightning Source LLC
LaVergne TN
LVHW051016080826
845145LV00009B/2656

* 9 7 8 1 6 4 6 6 2 7 5 9 2 *